THE
# INSTANT
# MILLIONAIRE

# THE
# INSTANT
# MILLIONAIRE

*A Tale of
Wisdom and
Wealth*

SECOND EDITION

# MARK FISHER
FOREWORD BY MARC ALLEN

New World Library
Novato, California

New World Library
14 Pamaron Way
Novato, California 94949

Author represented by the Cathy Miller Agency, London, UK
Edited by Katherine Dieter
Type design by Tona Pearce Myers

Library of Congress Cataloging-in-Publication Data
Fisher, Mark, date.
The instant millionaire : a tale of wisdom and wealth / Mark Fisher ; foreword by Marc Allen. — 2nd ed.
    p.    cm.
ISBN 978-1-57731-934-4 (pbk. : alk. paper)
1. Millionaires—Fiction. 2. Wealth—Fiction. I. Title.
PS3556.I8142I57 2010
813'.54—dc22                                         2010021997

First printing of second edition, August 2010
ISBN 978-1-57731-934-4
Printed in Canada on 100% postconsumer-waste recycled paper

New World Library is a proud member of the Green Press Initiative.

10  9  8  7  6  5  4  3  2  1

# CONTENTS

# FOREWORD

WE'RE ALL STORYTELLERS. We tell each other our stories, and we all love a good tale, whether it's in a movie, in a book, online, or whispered to us late at night.

We pass around our stories, and they include a vast number of fables. Fables are especially wonderful things because, as Webster defines it, they "enforce a useful truth." This little book presents us with a powerful and original fable that reveals one of the most useful truths of all: financial prosperity, and a fulfilling life well lived, are goals we can all achieve if we understand and *practice* the principles of success.

Perhaps a fable is the finest form in which to present these truths, for in the childlike simplicity of a fable, we can communicate directly with the childlike simplicity of our subconscious minds. Once we get a message to our subconscious minds, we can create a great many positive changes in our lives.

*The Instant Millionaire* has now been published in over thirty-seven editions all over the world, and over two million copies have been sold. The author is a genuine millionaire, and his little fable is not to be taken lightly.

This is a book to be read, reread, studied, and practiced. It is a brilliantly conceived book that can make you wealthy in many ways — and some are far more satisfying and valuable than material riches.

— Marc Allen
Author of *Visionary Business* and
*The Millionaire Course*

## CHAPTER ONE

## *In which the young man consults a wealthy relative*

THERE WAS ONCE A BRIGHT YOUNG MAN who wanted to get rich. He had had his fair share of disappointments and setbacks, it couldn't be denied, and yet he still believed in his lucky star.

While he waited for fortune to smile, he worked as an assistant to an account executive in a small advertising agency. He was inadequately paid and had felt for some time that his job offered him little satisfaction. His heart was simply no longer in it.

He dreamed of doing something else, perhaps writing a novel that would make him wealthy and famous and end his financial problems once and for all. But wasn't his ambition a bit unrealistic? Did he really have enough talent and technique to write a bestseller, or would the pages be filled with the bleak, unfocused ramblings of his inner misery?

His job had been a daily nightmare for more than a year. His boss spent most of each morning reading the newspaper and writing memos before disappearing to indulge in a three-hour lunch. He also changed his mind continually and gave contradictory orders.

But it wasn't only his boss — he was surrounded by colleagues who were also fed up with what they were doing. They seemed to have abandoned any sense of vision; they seemed to have given up altogether. He didn't dare tell any of them about his fantasy of dropping everything and becoming a writer. He knew they would treat it as a joke. When he was at work he often felt cut off from the world, as if he was in a foreign country, unable to speak the language.

Every Monday morning he wondered how on earth he was going to survive another week at the office. He felt totally alienated from the files piled high on his desk, from the needs of clients clamoring to sell their cigarettes, their cars, their beer....

He had written a letter of resignation six months earlier and had walked into his boss's office a dozen times with the letter burning in his pocket, but he had never been quite able to go through with it. It was funny; he would not have hesitated three or four years ago, but now he seemed unsure of what to do. Something was holding him back, some kind of force — or was it simply cowardice? He seemed to have lost the nerve that had always helped him get what he wanted in the past.

He kept waiting till the time was ripe, finding all kinds of excuses for not jumping into action, wondering if he could ever really succeed. Has he turned into a perpetual dreamer?

Did his paralysis spring from the fact that he was saddled with debts? Or was it because he had simply started to get old, a process inevitably triggered the minute we give up our visions of the future?

One day, when he was feeling especially frustrated, he suddenly thought of visiting an uncle of his who had become a millionaire. Perhaps he might be able to give him some advice, or better yet, some money.

His uncle was a warm, friendly person who immediately agreed to see him. He refused to lend him any money, however, claiming he wouldn't be doing him a favor.

"How old are you?" his uncle asked, after listening to his tale of woe.

"Thirty-two," the young man whispered timidly.

"Do you know that by the time J. Paul Getty was twenty-three he'd already made his first million? And that when I was your age, I had half a million? So how in the world is it that you are forced to borrow money at your age?"

"Beats me. I work like a dog, sometimes over fifty hours a week...."

"Do you really believe that hard work is what makes people rich?"

"I ... I guess so ... anyway, that's what I've always been led to believe."

"How much do you make a year — $35,000?"

"Yeah, about that much," replied the young man.

"Do you think that someone who earns $350,000 works ten times as many hours a week as you do? Obviously not! So if this person earns ten times more than you do without working any more than you do, then he must be doing something quite differently than you. He must have a secret you are totally unaware of."

"That must be true."

"You're lucky you understand that at least. Most people don't even get that far. They're far too busy trying to earn a living to stop and think about how they could get rid of their money problems. Most people don't even spend an hour of their time trying to figure out how they could get rich and why they've never managed to do so."

The young man had to admit that, despite his burning ambition and his dream of making a fortune, he had never taken the time to really think his situation through. Everything seemed to distract him and prevent him from facing up to a task that was obviously of fundamental importance.

The young man's uncle was silent for a while, then smiled.

"I've decided to help you out. I'm going to send you to the man who helped me get rich. He's called the Instant Millionaire. Have you heard of him?"

"No, never," the young man said.

"He chose that name because he claims he became a millionaire overnight after discovering the true secret of making a fortune. He claims he can help anyone become a millionaire overnight — or at least acquire the mentality of a millionaire."

His uncle turned to a large map on the wall and pointed to a small, somewhat isolated town.

"Have you ever been there?"

"No."

"Why not give it a try? Go and find him. He just

might reveal his secret to you. He lives in a fantastic house, the most beautiful one in the whole town. You shouldn't have any problem finding it."

"Why don't *you* just tell me the secret? Then I won't have to take the trouble of going there."

"Simply because I don't have the right to. When the Instant Millionaire confided it to me, the first thing he did was make me swear never to tell it to anybody. However, he did say I could refer people to him."

All of this seemed both surprising and involved to the young man. It certainly aroused his curiosity.

"Are you sure you can't tell me anything? Anything at all?"

"Absolutely positive. What I can do is recommend you highly to the Instant Millionaire."

The young man's uncle pulled out a sheet of elegant writing paper from a drawer in his massive oak desk, took his pen, and hastily scribbled a few lines. He then folded the letter, put it in an envelope, and handed it to his nephew.

"Here's your introduction," he said, "and here's the millionaire's address. One last thing. You must promise not to read this letter. If ever you *do* open it, despite my warning, and you still want it to work for you, you'll have to pretend that you haven't opened it. But how can you undo what's already been done?"

The young man didn't have the vaguest idea what his uncle was talking about, but he agreed. His uncle had always been a bit eccentric, and he was doing him a favor, after all, so he decided not to press the point. He thanked him warmly and left.

# CHAPTER TWO

## *In which the young man meets an elderly gardener*

THE YOUNG MAN SPED OFF toward the Instant Millionaire's town, his mind racing faster than his automobile. How hard was it going to be to meet this man? Would he welcome an unannounced visitor? Would he reveal his secret method of getting rich?

Just as he approached the millionaire's house, he was overcome by curiosity and, despite his uncle's words of warning, opened the letter of introduction.

He was shocked. His heart rate climbed and he broke into a sweat. He wondered whether his uncle had made a mistake or was playing a joke on him, because the "letter" was only a blank sheet of paper!

He was now at the gate of the millionaire's house and noticed a security guard. The guard had a stony expression; he looked as impenetrable as the enclosed fortress he was protecting.

"What can I do for you?" the guard asked drily.

"I'd like to meet the Instant Millionaire."

"Do you have an appointment?"

"No, but..."

"Well then, do you have a letter of introduction?"

The young man pulled the letter halfway out of his pocket and quickly stuffed it back in again.

"May I see your letter," the guard pressed.

The young man remembered his uncle's words, "If you open the letter, you must pretend that you haven't."

He handed the letter to the guard, who "read" it. His face remained totally expressionless.

"Fine," he said, as he gave the letter back to the young man. "You may come in."

The guard showed him where to park and led him to the front door of the millionaire's luxurious, Tudor-style home. An impeccably dressed butler opened the door.

"Can I help you?" he asked.

"I want to meet the Instant Millionaire."

"He's unable to see you at the moment. Please wait for him in the garden."

The butler accompanied the young man to the entrance of a garden with a glistening pond in the middle of it. He wandered in, admiring the beautiful flowers, bushes, and trees, and then he caught sight of a gardener who was bent over a rose bush. He must have been well into his seventies or eighties, and he wore a wide-brimmed straw hat that concealed his eyes.

When the young man approached him, the gardener broke off his work and welcomed him with a smile. He had bright, cheerful blue eyes.

"What have you come here for?" he asked in a warm and friendly voice.

"I've come to meet the Instant Millionaire."

"Oh, I see. And for what reason, if you don't mind my asking?"

"Well, I ... I'd simply like to ask him for advice...."

The gardener started to go back to his roses, then he stopped and turned. "Oh, by the way, you wouldn't have ten dollars on you, would you?"

"Ten dollars?" said the young man, blushing. "It's just that ... that's all I've got left on me."

"Perfect. That's all I need."

The gardener looked very dignified. His manner exuded exceptional grace and charm.

"I'd really like to give it to you," replied the young man, "but the problem is I wouldn't have any money left to get back home."

"Are you planning on going home today?"

"No-o-o... I mean, I've no idea," said the young man, now quite confused. "I don't want to leave until I've seen the Instant Millionaire."

"But if you don't need the money today, why are you so reluctant to lend it to me? You might not need it tomorrow. Who knows? You might be a millionaire."

The reasoning didn't sound completely logical to the young man, but he handed him the money. The gardener smiled.

"Most people are afraid of asking for things, and when they finally do, they don't insist enough. That's a mistake."

At that moment the butler arrived in the garden and spoke to the old man respectfully. "Sir, could you please let me have ten dollars? The cook's leaving today and insists on being paid. I'm just ten dollars short."

The gardener stuck his hand into his baggy pocket and pulled out a huge roll of bills. He must have had thousands of dollars in cash on him, because the young man caught sight of nothing but hundred-dollar bills, except for the ten-dollar bill on top. The gardener peeled off the bill he had just borrowed from the young man and handed it to the butler, who thanked him, bowed somewhat obsequiously, and quickly disappeared into the house.

The young man was outraged. How did the gardener have the gall to confiscate the last ten dollars he had in the world when his pockets were stuffed with more cash than he had ever seen?

"Why did you ask me for ten dollars?" he said, trying as hard as he could to conceal the rage he felt. "You didn't need it!"

"But of course I did. Look, I don't have any ten-dollar bills," he said, thumbing through the fat roll of cash. "You don't think I was going to give him a hundred, do you?"

"Why on earth do you keep so much money on you?"

"It's my pocket money," replied the gardener. "I always keep $25,000 on me in case of an emergency."

"Uh ... $25,000?" sputtered the young man, aghast.

Suddenly everything became clear: the ever-polite butler, that incredible amount of pocket money ...

"You're the Instant Millionaire, aren't you?"

"For the time being," replied the gardener. "I'm glad you've come.

"But tell me, how is it that you aren't rich yet? Have you ever seriously asked yourself that question?"

"Not really."

"Well, that's probably the first thing you should do. Think aloud in front of me, if you want. I'll try to follow your line of reasoning."

The young man made a few feeble attempts and then gave up.

"I see," said the millionaire. "You're not used to thinking out loud. Do you know there are lots of young people your age who are already rich? Some are even millionaires. Others are just on the verge of getting their first million. Did you know that when he was twenty-six, Aristotle Onassis already had $500,000 in the bank when he left for England, where he was planning to set up his shipping empire?"

"Only twenty-six?"

"That's right. And when he started out he had only a few hundred dollars to his name. He didn't have a university degree — and he didn't have any rich uncles.

"But now it's time for dinner. Would you like to join me?"

"Thank you very much. I'd love to."

The young man followed the millionaire, who,

despite his age, still had a lively bounce in his step. They went into the dining room, where the table had already been set for two.

"Please sit down." The millionaire pointed to the end of the table, the place usually reserved for the host. He sat to the right of his young guest, directly in front of a beautiful hourglass engraved with the motto *Time is Money*.

The butler arrived with a bottle of wine and filled their glasses.

"Let's drink to your first million," said the millionaire, raising his glass.

He took a sip, the only one he had all evening, and ate very modestly — just a few mouthfuls from a delicious salmon steak.

"Do you like what you do for a living?" the millionaire asked the young man.

"I suppose so. The situation in the office is a bit difficult."

"Make sure you're positive about your choice of careers. All the millionaires I've known — and I've met quite a few over the years — loved their occupations. For them, working became almost a leisure activity, as agreeable as a hobby. That's why most rich people rarely take vacations. Why should they deprive themselves of what they enjoy doing so much? And that's why they continue working even after becoming millionaires several times over.

"But though it's an absolute must to enjoy your work, it's not enough. To get rich, you have to know the secrets of wealth. Tell me, do you really believe these secrets exist?"

"Yes, I do."

"Good. That's the first step. Most people don't believe there are secrets to attaining wealth. They don't even believe they can become rich. And they're right, of course. If you don't think you can become rich, you very rarely do. You have to start by believing that you can, and then crave it passionately. Most people aren't ready to accept these secrets, even if they are revealed to them in very simple terms. Their greatest limitation is their own lack of imagination. That's why the true secrets of wealth are the best-kept secrets in the world.

"It's a little like the purloined letter in Edgar Allan Poe's story," the millionaire went on. "Do you remember it? It's the story about a letter the police were searching for and could never find, because, instead of being hidden away somewhere, it was lying in the least likely spot — in plain sight! Their lack of imagination and their built-in prejudices prevented the police from finding the letter. They weren't expecting to find it in plain sight, so they never saw it."

The young man listened to the millionaire with rapt attention. He was burning to find out what these secrets were. In any case, one thing was sure: Even if the millionaire didn't really have any secrets, he was certainly a master at setting an impressive scene.

# CHAPTER THREE

*In which the young man learns to seize opportunities and take risks*

"Now, HOW MUCH MONEY are you willing to pay to get these secrets of wealth?"

The millionaire's question took the young man by surprise.

"Even if I *was* willing to spend money to get it, I haven't got a dime."

"But *if* you had money, how much would you be willing to pay? Name a figure, any figure. The first one that comes to mind."

The young man couldn't possibly evade the question now. The millionaire was asking for a very specific answer.

"I don't know," he replied. "A hundred dollars...?"

The millionaire burst out laughing.

"Only a hundred dollars? Then you don't really believe these secrets exist, do you? If you did, you'd surely be ready to pay a lot more for them. Come on, I'll give you a second chance. Name another figure. This isn't a game, but a very serious matter."

The young man thought it over.

"I don't mind answering," he said. "But remember, I'm flat broke."

"Don't worry about that."

"But if I don't have any money, my hands are tied," said the young man, bewildered.

"Oh, my!" exclaimed the millionaire. "We've got a long way to go! Since time began, the rich have been using other people's money to amass their fortunes. Anyone really serious has never needed money to make money. By that I mean personal cash. Besides, you must have a checkbook on you...."

The young man wanted to deny it, but he had stuffed his checkbook into his pocket that morning. God knows why: he had exactly four dollars and twenty-eight cents in his account! He considered lying about it, but the millionaire had such a piercing gaze he seemed capable of mind-reading.

The young man heard himself stutter, as if he were confessing a deep, dark secret, "Yes, I br-brought it with me."

He pulled his checkbook out as automatically as a robot, even though an urge to rebel momentarily crossed his mind. He felt spellbound by this man, like someone in the hands of a hypnotist. Yet he wasn't afraid of the millionaire, for he radiated goodwill; he even seemed somewhat amused.

"Fine," replied the millionaire. "*Now* can you see there's no problem?"

He uncapped an elegant pen and handed it to the young man.

"Write out a check for the amount you have in mind and sign it."

"But I don't know how much to write."

"All right. Put down, say, $25,000."

The millionaire uttered this figure in a perfectly straightforward way, without a shred of arrogance.

"What . . . $25,000!" exclaimed the young man. "You've got to be joking."

"Put down $50,000 if you like," replied the millionaire, so calmly that the young man no longer knew whether he spoke seriously or in jest.

"Even $25,000 seems far too much. Anyway, you couldn't cash the check because it would just bounce. And all I'd get out of it would be an angry bank manager wondering whether I'd gone crazy. And he'd be right!"

"That's exactly how I undertook my biggest deal ever. I signed a check for $250,000 and then had to scramble around to find the money to cover it. But if I hadn't made out that check right then and there, I'd have missed an excellent opportunity.

"That was one of my first major business lessons," he said. "People who waste time waiting for all the perfect conditions to fall into place never get anything done. The ideal time for action is *now*!

"Another lesson this little exercise can teach you is this: If you want to succeed in life, you have to make sure you have no choice in the matter. You have to put your back to the wall. People who vacillate and refuse to take risks because they don't have all the elements in hand never get anywhere. The reason is simple. When you cut off all your exits and put your back to the wall, you mobilize all your inner powers. You want something to happen with every fiber of your being. So why hesitate now, young man? Put your back to the wall. Make out that $25,000 check to me."

The young man wrote out the check, slowly filling

in the numbers, then the words. But when he came to sign it, he simply couldn't do it.

"I've never written a check as large as this in my life."

"If you really want to become a millionaire, you'll have to start some day. You'll have to get used to signing checks much larger than this one. This is only the beginning."

But the young man still couldn't sign it. Everything was happening so quickly. He was about to hand over a check for $25,000 to a man he'd just met and who was promising some pretty dubious secrets in exchange.

"What's stopping you from signing?" asked the millionaire. "Everything's relative under the sun. In no time at all, this amount will appear insignificant to you."

"It's not the amount," mumbled the young man.

"Well, what is it, then? I know why you can't sign it. You don't really believe my secrets will turn you into a millionaire. If you were absolutely convinced, you'd sign in a flash. Tell me, if you were absolutely positive that these secrets would help you earn an additional $100,000 in less than a year, without your having to work harder than you do now — even by working less — would you sign that check?"

"Sure I would," he was forced to agree. "I'd make a $75,000 profit."

"So sign it. I guarantee that you'll be able to earn that amount."

"Would you be willing to put that in writing?"

The millionaire burst out laughing once again.

"I like you, young man. You're determined to cover your back. That's often a very prudent thing to do. Even if you're absolutely sure about your resources, it doesn't mean you should trust the first person who comes your way."

He left the table, rummaged about in a drawer, and pulled out a ready-made agreement. This didn't sit very well with the young man. Was the millionaire mass-producing his secrets and selling them to every Tom, Dick, and Harry who showed up?

The millionaire signed the guarantee and handed it to the young man, who skimmed over it quickly, satisfied with what he'd read. Then the old man suddenly changed his mind.

"I've got another idea," he said. "How about a bet?"

He took a coin from his pocket and bounced it up and down in the palm of his hand.

"Let's play heads or tails. If I lose, I'll give you the $25,000 cash I have in my pocket. If I win, you give me the check. In either case, let's forget about the guarantee."

"The only problem," the young man said, "is what I told you. There's almost nothing in my account. Even if I give you this check, you won't be able to cash it."

"No problem," said the millionaire. "I'm in no hurry. Why not postdate it a year from now?"

The young man hesitated.

"All right. Under those conditions I accept the bet."

He had now calculated that in any event he had a full year to change banks, close his account, or simply stop the check. He had nothing to lose. And with the millionaire's new offer he could even earn $25,000 in a few seconds flat, without having to do an ounce of work!

A self-satisfied smile flitted across his lips. He hoped the millionaire hadn't noticed it.

The millionaire then proposed a minor clarification, which immediately confirmed the young man's doubts.

"There's just one thing. You have to solemnly swear that, should you lose the bet, you'll still honor this check."

The young man tentatively gave his word, but just as the millionaire was about to toss the coin, he abruptly interrupted him.

"May I see the coin?" he asked.

The millionaire smiled.

"No doubt about it. I really like you, young man. You're cautious. That'll help you avoid a lot of mistakes. Just make sure it doesn't cause you to miss out on a lot of good opportunities."

The millionaire handed over the coin. As soon as the young man had carefully examined both sides and returned it, the millionaire asked him to call.

"Tails."

The millionaire tossed the coin, and the young man's heart began to beat as wildly as if he were on his first date! This was the first time he'd ever had the chance of winning $25,000!

As he watched the coin spinning in the air, his anxiety mounted sharply. The coin landed on the table.

"Heads!" said the millionaire gleefully, but then quickly added a sympathetic, "Sorry."

It was hard to say wether he was being sincere or merely polite.

The young man couldn't help trembling a little as he signed the check. He would probably get used to signing big checks like this one day, but at this point it made him feel very strange indeed.

He gave the check to the millionaire, who examined it briefly, folded it, and put it in his pocket.

"Now," said the young man, "can I have the secrets?"

"But of course," said the millionaire. "Do you

have a piece of paper? I'll write them down for you. That way, you won't forget them."

The young man had a hard time grasping his words. The millionaire surely couldn't expect a single sheet of paper to hold all the secrets — especially secrets he'd just bought for $25,000!

"Sorry. I don't have any paper on me."

"But didn't you have a letter of introduction when you arrived here? The people your uncle has sent me over the years always had a letter."

The young man took it out of his pocket.

He handed it over, carefully watching the old man's face as he opened it. But the millionaire didn't seem at all surprised to find it was completely blank. He took his pen, leaned over the table, and was about to write something when he raised his head and asked the young man to fetch the butler.

"You'll find him in the kitchen, at the far end of that corridor over there," explained the millionaire.

When the young man came back with the butler, the millionaire was sealing the envelope. He seemed pleased with himself.

"Our young guest will be spending the night," he said to the butler. "Would you take him to his room, please?"

Then he turned to the young man and said, "Here are the secrets." He stood up and handed him the envelope; then he solemnly shook his hand, as if he had just wrapped up one of the most important deals he had ever made in his life.

"The only thing I must ask you to do is to wait until you're alone in your room before opening the envelope and reading the secrets. And oh, there's one more condition. Before you may read what I've written, you must promise to spend part of your life sharing these secrets with those less fortunate than you. If you agree, you'll be the last person to whom I'll ever give these secrets directly. My work here will be over. I'll be ready to take care of roses in a much larger garden.

"If you don't feel ready to share these secrets," he said, "you still have time to back out. But then, of course, you won't be able to open the envelope. I'll give you back your check. And you'll be free to go home and get on with the same life you've been leading up to now."

Now that the young man finally had his hands on the letter containing the secrets, there was no possibility of backing out. His curiosity had gotten the better of him.

"I promise," he replied.

# CHAPTER FOUR

## *In which the young man finds himself a prisoner*

SOON THE YOUNG MAN WAS ALONE IN HIS ROOM, a room so luxurious he couldn't help examining it. He went up to the only window, which was very high off the ground, and looked out over the park. He could see where he had first spotted the millionaire looking after his roses with such tender, loving care.

Night had fallen, and a full moon cast a luminescent glow over everything. He was filled with anticipation. He was finally going to discover the secrets to making the fortune that had eluded him for so many years.

He slowly opened the envelope and unfolded the letter. The sheet of paper was again completely blank! He turned it over. There wasn't the tiniest squiggle on either side. He's been fool enough to let the old man swindle him! He'd handed over a check for a mind-boggling sum in exchange for something that didn't exist!

The millionaire had seemed so honest. He'd even started feeling fond of the old man.

The young man realized that he should have been more careful, that perhaps there was some truth after all in the belief that totally honest people never get rich. He was forced to admit that he had no business sense at all — probably the very reason he was still poor. And now even poorer! A feeling of rebellion engulfed him and he crumpled up the paper and threw it across the room.

What could he do? He'd let himself be lured into a well-sprung trap. He had only one alternative: to leave as quickly as possible. Who knows? Maybe his life was in danger, too. He didn't want to spend the night in this place.

He decided the best thing to do would be to sneak out as quietly as possible. He tiptoed to the door and slowly turned the handle, but the door was bolted from the outside. The window was the only other exit, and it was about thirty feet above the ground. If he jumped, he'd surely break his neck. His only option was to ring for the butler.

He pulled the bell and waited. No one came.

He rang again. Nothing. Maybe the bell was out of order.

The house was totally silent. He was a prisoner.

He lay on the bed and the events of the day raced before his eyes. There was little he could do to fight off the feeling of absurdity that was beginning to overwhelm him. The blank sheet of paper he had bought for $25,000 kept drifting before him, as if bent on mocking him.

Sleep finally overtook him. He dreamed of a stranger luring him repeatedly to sign a thick document of the utmost importance, as if his life depended on it. He protested vehemently. There must be some mistake — the document was totally blank. . . .

# CHAPTER FIVE

## *In which the young man learns to have faith*

THE NEXT MORNING the young man felt as if he'd been run over by a three-ton truck.

He glanced at himself in the mirror. He had slept in his clothes and looked awful but it only bolstered his determination. He had one thought in mind: to find the old man, give him back his "secret," and get his check back.

He ran his fingers through his hair and headed toward the door, recalling it had been locked the night before. It wasn't now. He strode out angrily and headed for the dining room.

He found the millionaire sitting calmly at the table, dressed in the same clothes he'd had on the day before: clean but surprisingly threadbare gardener's clothes. His large, pointed, wide-brimmed hat was lying in front of him on the table.

The millionaire was flipping a coin in the air and counting as it landed on the table.

"Nine," he muttered without taking his eyes off the coin.

"Ten . . . damn!" He lifted his head.

"I've never been able to go beyond ten," he said. "I get what I want ten times in a row and then invariably it fails on the eleventh throw, even though I toss it exactly the same way each time."

The young man realized he had been duped the night before.

"My father, who was an accomplished magician, would regularly get to fifteen," said the millionaire. "I didn't inherit his talent."

The young man asked to see the coin. The millionaire cheerfully gave it to him, and the young man flipped it onto the table. Heads. Tails. Heads. Tails. It obviously wasn't a trick coin, unless there was some secret mechanism that escaped his notice.

"There was nothing dishonest about our bet

yesterday," said the millionaire. "I simply displayed my skill at handling money. Some people take skillfulness for dishonesty, but they're two very different things."

The young man brandished the letter and threw it on the table.

"You did a fine job of tricking me, sir. You made yourself some easy money there: $25,000 for a blank sheet of paper."

"It's the secret of wealth," the millionaire said.

"Well, you're going to have to explain yourself. Do you take me for an idiot?"

"An idiot? Of course not. You're simply lacking in insight. It's quite normal. Your mind is still immature."

"Maybe it is, but I can certainly recognize a blank piece of paper when I see one."

"I assure you that you can become very rich indeed with just this blank piece of paper. That's all I needed to become an instant millionaire way back when. But since I must soon go back to tend my beloved roses, I'll help you. Listen carefully, because as soon as you apply this secret successfully, you'll have to share it with others. Once you've freed yourself of the shackles of poverty, you'll have to show the way to those still bound hand and foot. May I ask you to repeat the promise you made yesterday?"

There was no doubt about it; the millionaire was an extraordinarily persuasive man. Just a few minutes before the young man had been ready to curse him and now he was listening attentively.

He repeated his promise.

"I must warn you that becoming a millionaire will probably seem too easy. But don't let simplicity deceive you. Each time you begin to have doubts, remember Mozart: true genius resides in simplicity. You'll tend to have doubts in the beginning. With time, as wealth is magnetically attracted to you in a most unexpected way, you'll begin to understand."

"That's exactly what I've been hoping for with all my heart: to understand!"

"So much the better. Once you've grasped this secret, you'll know why you believe in it. But in the beginning, despite its simplicity, this secret will seem so surprising that you'll be incapable of understanding it — or even believing it, for that matter. So I have to ask you to make a small leap of faith. If the secret exists, you'll have gained everything because of your faith. If it doesn't, you won't have lost a thing."

# CHAPTER SIX

## *In which the young man learns to focus on a goal*

"FEEL FREE TO ASK ME ANY QUESTIONS that cross your mind," said the millionaire. "It'll be a pleasure for me to answer them. Soon you won't be able to do so. Our time together is limited, so let's not waste it in futile discussions. Here's a pen. Do you have the piece of paper?"

"Here it is."

"Do you really want to become rich?"

"I most certainly do."

"All right, then. Write down the amount of money you want and how much time you'll allow yourself to acquire it."

"Do you think money's going to drop like pennies from heaven just because I write a couple of numbers down on paper?"

"Yes, I do," said the millionaire. "I warned you that the secret would be simple. All the millionaires I've met told me they became rich the moment they set themselves an amount and a deadline by which to acquire it. If you don't know where you're heading, the chances are you'll never get anywhere."

"It sounds like magic to me."

"But that's exactly what it is — the magic of a *quantified objective*.

"Let's look at the problem from a different angle. Suppose you're trying to get a job. You go through all the necessary steps and finally get an interview. A short while later, you're told that you're being seriously considered. Then you find out you've got the job and that you'll be making a lot of money. How would you react? For a start, you'd be really pleased with yourself. Being chosen from dozens, perhaps hundreds, of candidates — what a feat! And since you were unemployed for, say, three months, you'd think this was a very lucky break indeed. But once your initial euphoria had passed, what would be your next reaction?"

"Well, I'd wonder when the job would start. Then, I'd like to know the exact meaning of 'a lot of money.' All things being relative, I'd try to find out exactly how much the salary was going to be and what kind of benefits would be offered."

"Good! If, for example, you asked your new boss what he meant by 'a lot of money' and all he was willing to do was guarantee that you would definitely earn a lot, you wouldn't be satisfied, would you? Worse yet, you'd probably start having second thoughts about his honesty. The fact that he refused to name a specific figure could quite possibly mean that there was something shady going on, and that your salary wasn't going to be as generous as he'd been implying. And if he refused to tell you the exact date you were supposed to start the job, you would really be suspicious, wouldn't you? You'd try to pin him down."

"I suppose I would," agreed the young man.

"And if you insisted on it and still couldn't get the details you wanted, you might just turn it down and start looking elsewhere. In fact, you'd be fully justified in doing so."

"You're right. The offer leaves a lot to be desired."

The millionaire looked content. He paused a moment before proceeding, his lips still set in a teasing but good-natured smile.

"The questions you asked your potential employer were aimed at getting hard facts. Right? Just knowing that you were going to earn a lot of money wasn't enough. You also wanted to know how much. Finding out that you'd been given the job didn't satisfy you, either. You also wanted to know the exact starting date. And you'd probably want all of this in writing, because a contract adds backbone to a verbal agreement. Spoken words are ephemeral but the written word is permanent.

"What most people, or at least the unsuccessful ones, are unaware of is that life gives us exactly what we ask from it. The first thing to do, therefore, is to ask for exactly what you want. If your request is vague, whatever you get will be just as muddled. If you ask for the minimum, you'll get the minimum.

"Any request you make must be absolutely precise. As far as monetary wealth is concerned, you must establish an amount and a deadline by which to make it. What do people generally do? Even those who want money and lots of it all make the same mistake: they don't establish an exact amount and a deadline by which to make it. If you need convincing, just ask someone exactly how much money he wants to earn next year. Ask him to reply right away. If this person is really on the road to success, if he really knows where he's going, and if he doesn't mind confiding in you, he'll be able to answer immediately. Nine out of ten people, however, will be incapable of answering this simple question off the top of their heads. It is the most common mistake. Life wants to know exactly what you expect from it. If you don't ask for anything, you won't get anything.

"Now let's test you," the old man said. "You told me you'd like to get rich."

"Definitely."

"Tell me how much you'd like to earn next year."

The young man found himself at a loss for words. He had had no trouble following the old man's line of reasoning. In fact, he had agreed with it wholeheartedly. And yet he had to admit that he belonged to the vast majority of people who want to get rich but don't know how much they want to make. He was embarrassed.

"I don't know," he was forced to admit. "But I think I've just understood one of my mistakes — perhaps the most fundamental one."

"It is a serious mistake. Let's try to correct it. Come on, write down the amount you have in mind."

"I really don't have the vaguest idea," muttered the young man.

"And yet it's so easy. Write down the amount you'd like to earn in the next year. I know what we'll do. Take a few minutes to think it over. When the time's up, you've *got* to write down an amount. We've already established the deadline: one year from today. So all you have to think about is the amount. Get going! Time's slipping away!"

As he said this, he picked up the golden hourglass on the table and turned it over.

The young man quickly got into the spirit of the game, and realized it was the first time he'd had to concentrate so hard in his life. All sorts of numbers flitted about uncontrollably in his head. Time was running out. When the last grain of sand had fallen, he still hadn't settled on a specific figure.

"Good," said the millionaire, who hadn't taken his eyes away from the hourglass. "What figure do you have in mind?"

The young man finally picked the most expansive figure he thought he was capable of making, and slowly wrote down the numbers.

"Only $75,000!" exclaimed the millionaire. "That's pretty low — but it's a start. I would have preferred $500,000. You've got quite a lot of work to do before becoming an instant millionaire. But you'll see; it won't be as tiring as most people imagine it to be. And it'll be the most important work you'll ever do in your life, no matter what occupation you end up choosing. It's called working on *yourself*."

# CHAPTER SEVEN

*In which the young man gets
to know the value of self-image*

THE BUTLER CAME INTO THE DINING ROOM carrying coffee and croissants, and the young man ate while the lesson continued.

"I'm going to ask you a series of questions," said the millionaire, "to help you understand what happened to you during your few minutes of reflection.

"The first thing you must realize is that the amount you wrote down on that piece of paper means much more than you think it does. In fact, that amount represents almost to a penny what you think you're worth. In your eyes, whether you are willing to admit it or not, you're worth $75,000 a year. Not a penny more and not a penny less."

"I don't see how you can say that," said the young man. "The fact that I chose that particular amount means I'm level-headed and have both feet on the ground. I just can't see how I can earn more for the time being. After all, I don't have a very high-paying job, or a degree, or anything in the bank."

"Your way of thinking is valid to an extent. In any case, I respect it. The only problem is, this attitude is the cause of your current situation. External circumstances are not really very important. Keep this well in mind: *All the events in your life are a mirror image of your thoughts.* Your mind can't grasp this principle if you continue to accept the widespread illusion that external factors determine your life. In reality, everything in life is a matter of attitude. Life is exactly as you picture it. Everything that happens to you is a product of your thoughts. So if you want to change your life, you must start by changing your thoughts. No doubt you consider this a bit trite. Many 'rational' individuals stubbornly refute this principle.

"But the truth is, all those who have accomplished great things in life, regardless of the field, have always ignored the objections raised by strictly 'rational' thinkers.

"This certainly doesn't mean I'm against intelligence in any way. Quite the contrary. Reasoning and logic are essential in order to achieve success. But they aren't enough. They must be instruments and faithful servants, nothing more.

"In most cases reasoning and logic become roadblocks in the way of great achievement, because great things are created only by those who have faith in the powers of the mind. Successful people never let circumstances bother them too much. When you come down to it, the circumstances facing great achievers in the past were just as difficult as — and often even more difficult than — those facing their contemporaries, but this simply caused them to reach even deeper to tap their inner strength. Those achievers firmly believed that they could accomplish great things. All those who became rich were deeply convinced that they could get rich. And that's why they succeeded.

"But let's get back to our piece of paper and answer this question: The $75,000 figure you wrote down was surely not the largest one that came to your mind, was it?"

"You're right. It wasn't."

"What was, then?"

"My head was crowded with so many numbers...."

"For instance?"

"Well, $100,000."

"And why didn't you write it down?"

"I don't know. I suppose it seemed totally out of reach."

"It'll remain that way until you believe you can reach it.

"Since you started with only $75,000, we've got a big job ahead of us; and if we don't do it, it'll take you a very long time to become a millionaire. So write down the highest figure that now seems achievable to you. Stretch yourself."

After a moment of reflection, the young man wrote down $100,000.

"Congratulations," the millionaire responded quickly. "You've just earned $25,000 in a few seconds. Not bad, eh?"

"I haven't earned it yet."

"It's as if you had. You've taken the biggest step. You expanded your self-image by considering you could earn $100,000 instead of $75,000. It's not a major leap forward, but it's progress all the same. Rome wasn't built in a day, after all.

"Inside you lies a kind of Rome — as it does in every human being. The astonishing thing is that this city is both exactly as you picture it, and it's also surprisingly flexible. The size of your city depends on the exact circumference you give it. By increasing the figure you wrote down, you expanded your city limits. Your inner Rome grew, and it's just a beginning.

"All wise thinkers have said for ages that the greatest limitations are those man imposes on himself, and thus the greatest obstacle to success is a mental obstacle. Expand your mental limits and you will expand the limits of your life. Explode your limitations and you will explode the limitations of your life. The conditions in your life will change as if by magic. I swear by experience this is true."

"But how can I find out what my mental limitations are?" the young man asked. "All this seems plausible, yet at the same time quite abstract."

"I've just explained how to find the boundary that corresponds to your self-image," said the millionaire. "You translated it into concrete terms when you wrote down that number. It's fascinating to see what each individual really thinks of himself. Each time someone does this exercise, a single figure immediately exposes his true self-image. He is confronted by his mental limitations, which will perfectly match the limits he encounters in life. Life will bow before the limits he sets for himself — whether he is aware of this or not. People who generally fail are the least conscious of these key principles of success and wealth. Successful individuals have become aware of this phenomenon and have done their utmost to work on their self-image.

"The easiest way to work on this self-image in the beginning is to take a blank sheet of paper and write down steadily increasing amounts. Let's start our little exercise over again. Write down a much bolder figure this time."

The young man thought for a few seconds and, squirming, wrote down $150,000, confessing that this was the maximum he could imagine earning.

"Maybe it's the maximum you can imagine, but it's definitely not the maximum you could *actually* earn. That's a pretty modest figure. Some people earn it in a month, others in a week, even a day — every day of the year. However, let me congratulate you. You've made astounding progress: you've doubled your earnings and considerably extended your mental boundaries — not as much as I would like, but I don't want to rush you. You have to start by setting yourself an objective that you consider bold but at the same time reasonable.

"The secret of any goal is that it must be both ambitious *and* within reach. But don't forget that most people are overly conservative — they're afraid to burst through their mental limitations. They've turned their mental limitations into a kind of habit. They're used to going without. They're convinced that's what life's all about. They're scared to dream.

"You mustn't be afraid of expanding your mental boundaries. What you can accomplish in an hour, merely by writing down a series of larger and larger numbers, is amazing. You've managed to double your goal within a matter of a few minutes. Later on, when you're alone, do the next exercise. Sit down in the privacy of your own room and write out the course of your financial destiny. This is how to do it. Write: *In six years to the day I will be a millionaire*. This is the practical application of my secret to becoming an instant millionaire. You'll probably object to the fact that it'll take you six long years to become a millionaire. I agree, but it'll take you only a second to activate the secret key that will ensure your financial destiny and fortune.

"As for me, I started out with some cash that an old millionaire lent me — equivalent to about $25,000 in today's dollars — and it took me precisely five years and nine months to make my first million. Ever since then, I've made it prosper by using the same formula over and over, with ever-increasing numbers. This formula has always made some people laugh, and that's not going to change. However, the ones who laugh aren't rich!"

The young man shook his head pensively. He was half convinced. But it all seemed a bit too easy.

"Obviously," continued the millionaire, "this formula is effective for those who want to become something other than millionaires. After all, not everyone cherishes that ambition. And that's precisely the beauty of this secret. It works equally well for any dream — from the most modest to the most extravagant. It can make you an extra $5,000 a year or double your income in a year — something that's totally feasible, by the way.

"So, if you don't mind, go and spend some time in your room while I go back to my precious roses, and write the sentence I gave you: *In six years to the day, I will be a millionaire. I will therefore be a millionaire on*, and then write the month, the day, and the year. Make sure you take note of every impression that comes into your mind, no matter what it may be. You'll find some paper in the desk. Remember one thing: As long as you aren't used to the idea of becoming a millionaire, as long as it isn't an integral part of your life and thus of your innermost thoughts, nothing can help you become a millionaire.

"Go now and reflect on my formula or affirmation, as you may wish to call it. Let it become your guiding principle during the next six years."

## CHAPTER EIGHT

### *In which the young man discovers the power of words*

A<small>N HOUR LATER</small> the butler came to fetch the young man, who had been so engrossed in the exercise the eccentric millionaire had given him to do, that it seemed as if no time at all had passed.

The butler explained that the millionaire was expecting him in the garden, and he accompanied the young man there in silence. His host was sitting on a bench, contemplating a freshly cut rose. He raised his head when he heard the young man approach. A gentle smile lit his face. He was radiant; in fact, he seemed almost ecstatic.

"So, how did it go?" he asked. "Did the exercise work out all right?"

"Yes, it did. But I've got a lot of questions."

"That's what I'm here for."

He invited the young man to sit next to him.

"What bothers me in particular," he told the old man, "is that I just can't see how I can become a millionaire in six years even if I do write down this crazy sentence and meditate on it. How can I *convince* myself that I can become a millionaire? I don't even know which field I want to work in. And I still feel I'm pretty young to become a millionaire."

"Youth is no obstacle. Countless people became rich at a much younger age than yours. The major obstacle is not knowing the secret, or knowing it and not applying it."

"I feel ready to apply it. But the only trouble is that I don't think I can *honestly* convince myself that I can become a millionaire."

"There's basically only one way to do it. And it's the same method you use to persuade yourself that you *can't* become a millionaire even if you want to.

"During the next few days, or few weeks at the most, you are going to develop the attitude of an instant millionaire. Naturally, it's going to take some time to undo everything you've built up over the years.

"The secret to developing this personality resides in words, combined with images, which are the special way in which thoughts express themselves. Each thought you have tends to manifest itself in your life in one way or another. The stronger a person's character is, the more powerful his thoughts will be, and the more quickly they will tend to manifest, thus shaping the circumstances of his life. This undoubtedly inspired the early Greek philosopher Heraclitus to observe, 'Character equals destiny.'

"Desire is what best sustains your thoughts. The more passionate your desire is, the more quickly the thing you want will spring up in your life. The way to become rich is to desire it fervently. In every area of life, sincerity and fervor are necessary ingredients of success."

"And yet I sincerely wish to be rich," said the young man. "I've been doing everything possible for years now. But nothing's worked out."

"Ardent desire is necessary, but not enough. What you lack is faith. You must *believe* that you will become a millionaire."

"How can I get this faith?"

"I've read a great many books on this subject. And

what my own mentor taught me corresponds to the conclusions reached in them: *The way to obtain faith is through the repetition of words*. Words have an extraordinary impact on our inner and outer lives. Words are omnipotent. Most people are totally unaware of this principle and fail to use it — no, I take that back. They do use the power of words, but generally to their detriment."

"I don't want to contradict you," said the young man, "but I think you're exaggerating. I can't really see how words can help me become a millionaire. They have some importance, but certainly other things are more important, and more powerful."

The millionaire didn't respond. He was absorbed in his own thoughts for a moment. Then he said, "In the desk up in your room I left a booklet that explains this theory in a very enlightening way. Go and find it. It's very short. Read it and come down again. We'll continue our discussion then."

The young man went back to his room, closed the door, and searched for the booklet in the desk. There was no booklet, but he found a letter that was apparently addressed to him even though it didn't have his name written on it. It was inscribed, *Letter to a Young Millionaire*.

He opened it. It contained a single word written in red ink: FAREWELL. It was signed, *The Instant Millionaire*.

The young man's heart began to flutter like a butterfly gone mad. At that moment he heard a strange sound behind him. He turned around and saw a computer he had not previously noticed. He approached it and saw that a single sentence, repeated over and over again, filled the screen:

YOU HAVE AN HOUR LEFT TO LIVE.
YOU HAVE AN HOUR LEFT TO LIVE.
YOU HAVE AN HOUR LEFT TO LIVE.
YOU HAVE AN HOUR LEFT TO LIVE.

If this was a joke, it was certainly in bad taste. It had to be a joke, though. Why would the Instant Millionaire want him to die? The young man hadn't done anything to him. But everything was so strange in this place. Maybe the millionaire was a madman hiding his murderous tendencies behind a veneer of kindheartedness.

The young man was terribly confused. He was sure of one thing, however: whether or not this was a joke, he wasn't going to take any risks. He was going to make his escape, and forget about his check and the magical theories the millionaire had used to fuel his gullible imagination.

He threw the letter on the floor and made for the door, but again it was firmly locked. He was overwhelmed with panic. He shook the handle, trying to force the door open, but it was hopeless.

The young man went wild. He ran to the window and saw the millionaire working in the garden. He shouted to him. No answer. He screamed more frantically. Again no answer. The butler stepped into the garden, and the young man called out to him in a hysterical voice. But it was as if his shouts didn't exist.

What kind of horrible nightmare was he going through?

He called again and again. Another servant appeared a few paces behind the butler. He, too, was completely oblivious to the prisoner's screams for help. The young man became more and more desperate.

He frantically searched for something with which to pry open the door. As he passed the window, he noticed a man approaching the house. He was wearing an immense black cloak and a wide-brimmed black hat. The young man's chest was constricted; he was almost suffocating with terror. Who could it be but a hired assassin coming to get him? It was clear. He was trapped. He was going to die.

Soon he heard heavy footsteps slowly making their way toward the door. He was right. His time had finally come. He searched left and right for something, anything, with which to defend himself, but could find nothing. He heard the key turning in the lock. The handle moved; the door opened.

Standing in the doorway was a murky black shadow, which swiftly turned into the more substantial figure of a man, standing silently, motionless as a statue. Then the man plunged his hand into his pocket. The young man thought he was going to pull out a weapon, but the mysterious stranger drew out a piece of paper instead. He lifted the brim of his hat and the young man, breathlessly expecting the worst, saw it was the millionaire.

"You forgot the figures you came up with in the garden," said the millionaire. "Did you find the booklet I told you about?"

"No, I didn't. I found this instead," the young man said angrily.

He retrieved the letter from the floor.

"What's the meaning of this grotesque scenario you just played out?" the young man said. "I could sue you, you know."

"But...they're only words, a word scribbled on a piece of paper, a few words on a computer screen.

Didn't you tell me that you didn't believe in the power of words? Look at the state you're in. . . ."

The young man suddenly realized what the millionaire was talking about.

"I just wanted to give you a quick lesson. Experience is a much better teacher than mere theory. Experience is life. Wasn't that Goethe's philosophy? Gray is the color of theory; green, the color of the tree of life.

"Now do you understand the power that words have? Their power is so great they don't even need to be true to have an effect on people. I assure you I did not at any time have criminal intentions toward you."

"How was I to know that?" said the young man, gradually calming down.

"You could have used your head and reasoned things out. Why on earth would I want to kill you? You've never done me any harm. Even if you had, I would never waste time on revenge. All I want is to be free to tend my rose garden.

"You should have relied on your sense of logic. Yet, did you notice how powerless logic is in a situation such as this? When you were shouting to us from the window and we were pretending not to hear, you were truly in despair. The mistake you made was not in reading the words, but in believing them. By doing so you instinctively obeyed one of the greatest laws governing the human mind: When imagination and logic are in conflict with each other, the imagination invariably takes over."

## CHAPTER NINE

*In which the young man is first
shown the heart of the rose*

"YOU'VE LEARNED MANY IMPORTANT THINGS today," the millionaire told the young man. "And hopefully you've understood them not only with your head but with your heart as well.

"Now you know that words deeply affect our lives whether we wish them to or not. A thought, even when false, can affect us if we believe it to be true. When you learn to distinguish the value of a thought, that is, the value you give it, your mind can regain or maintain its calm. It was your mind that gave meaning to the threat. If it had been written in a foreign language, you wouldn't have paid the slightest attention to it."

The millionaire was silent for a moment, then continued.

"In the future, each time you come face-to-face with a problem — and the road to fortune is strewn with obstacles — remember this particular threat. Remind yourself that the problem facing you has as little to do with you as this threat did. This might seem unrealistic to you, since you're the one who has to deal with the problem. But you don't have to shoulder the anxiety it breeds, or let a problem acquire so much importance that it traumatizes you. By the time you have reached this point — and it's not easy, I assure you — you will have mastered an invaluable skill and will be able to fulfill all your dreams.

"Let me warn you, however. The journey may be long and arduous before you manage to master it. But never give up. I promise you, it'll be worth your while. One day you will learn that mastering your destiny and fulfilling your dreams is the ultimate purpose of life. The rest is unimportant."

They both remained silent, absorbed in their thoughts. The young man noticed the millionaire's eyes filling with sadness. . . .

The millionaire continued, as if summing up everything he had said up to that point: "Life can be a rose garden or hell on earth, depending on your frame of mind. Think of the rose often. Lose yourself in the heart of a rose each time a problem crops up. And remember, you don't have to shoulder the burden of your problems."

He placed particular emphasis on the following words: "Most people cannot understand what I've just said. They believe it to be pure, unadulterated optimism. But it's much more profound than that. The world is but a reflection of your inner self. The conditions in your life are but a mirror image of your inner life. Concentrate on the heart of the rose and there you will find truth and the intuition you will need to guide you through life.

"You will also find the dual secret of true wealth: love for whatever you do, and love for others."

# CHAPTER TEN

*In which the young man learns
to master his unconscious mind*

AFTER THIS LONG AND HEARTFELT STATEMENT the old millionaire seemed exhausted, and became silent for several minutes. Then he continued, carefully stressing each word.

"The formula, or affirmation, I have given you is so powerful. Even if in the beginning you believe it highly unlikely you will ever become a millionaire, you *will* be able to become one. Just do the same thing with the formula that you did with the message on the computer — accept it as the truth. If you have faith that you will be able to accomplish something, you will."

"In the case of the computer," the young man said, "I let myself be tricked. I lost my head. But this formula is a different matter altogether — I have a problem believing I can become a millionaire six years from now."

"Even if you don't believe in the formula now, it'll begin acting on you. The more you internalize it, the more powerful it becomes. It's not your reasoning or *conscious* mind that you must convince. Remember the threat. Part of you — your imagination — accepted it as real. And the imagination is what some people call the *unconscious* mind. It is the hidden part of your mind, and much more powerful than the conscious part. It guides your entire life. I could spend hours talking to you about the theory of the unconscious. But it's enough for you to know that the unconscious is extremely susceptible to the power of words. Now do you know why you are having so much difficulty believing the undeniable fact that you can become a millionaire in less than six years?"

"Sorry. I don't."

"Well, the fact remains that for years and years you've been telling yourself you can't. Words have been engraving themselves in your unconscious. Deeply. In fact, every experience, every thought you've ever had, every word you've ever heard has become indelibly etched in your unconscious. In the long run, this prodigious memory becomes your self-image. Without realizing it, your past experiences and your inner monologue have convinced you that you aren't the type of person who can become a millionaire, even if, objectively speaking, you have all the qualities to do so, and you could do so, more easily than you can imagine. Your self-image, like everyone else's, is so powerful that it unwittingly becomes your destiny. Outer circumstances end up matching the image you have of yourself with amazing precision. To become rich, you have to create a new self-image."

"Perhaps I can. I'm quite willing to try. The only snag is that I'm not really sure where to start."

"Think about the threat you experienced. It wasn't real, yet it affected you as if it was. All you have to do is play the same trick on yourself. Your unconscious won't be any the wiser for it. Think about it: from childhood on, each suggestion you have accepted, whether true or false, in effect has tricked your unconscious. You may have accepted something that was patently untrue. So now you're going to experience the same thing. Your unconscious can be influenced at will; it is as easy as child's play. And once it has been influenced in the way you want it to be, you will be able to obtain exactly what you want out of life. Why? Because your unconscious will be convinced that you *can* obtain all these things. It will accept them as true in the same way that it's now accepting the fact that you can't get more out of life. This ties in with what I said earlier. Man is the reflection of the thoughts stored in his unconscious.

"The most important thing is to pretend, as best you can, that something is true. Why does this work with the unconscious? Simply because, though the unconscious may be powerful, it cannot discriminate between truth and falsehood."

"Yes, but what happens if there's a conflict between my conscious and unconscious? What happens if my conscious mind refuses to accept the idea of wealth?"

"The best solution is *repetition*. This technique is commonly called self-suggestion. Each one of us is subject to it throughout our lives. Every day we are influenced by inner and outer suggestions. The inner monologue that all of us live with continually shapes our lives. Some of us repeat to ourselves that we will never be successful because we come from a family of losers, or because we have had failures, or because we think we haven't had enough education, or don't have enough money, or skills, or intelligence, or management ability, or good luck; and on and on it goes. So we drift from failure to failure, not because we don't have the necessary qualities to succeed, but because that's how we unconsciously picture ourselves.

"Some people believe they will never attract a partner," the millionaire continued. "And yet they have all kinds of attractive qualities. Potential partners run from them like the plague. The power of their self-image, which is the reflection of the unconscious, is responsible for this. It brings about the circumstances that make others avoid them.

"But the repetition of negative formulas, which have such a tremendous impact on our lives, can be used in a different way. And that's what we're going to do. The unconscious is a slave that can dominate us because it is immensely powerful. But it is also blind, and you have to learn how to play tricks on it."

The young man didn't fully understand everything the millionaire was saying, yet he was eager to find out more.

"The beauty of this theory is that you don't really have to believe in it to use it," the millionaire said. "But to get results you have to put it to use: they won't come magically on their own. Everything, as I've said, depends on repetition. Even if you don't believe it at first, try it — at least for a couple of days. That's long enough for you to start feeling its effects.

"This might seem simplistic, but let me tell you it is the most potent secret on the face of the earth. Words have tremendous power. Remember the first words of St. John in the Bible: 'In the beginning was the Word.' Self-suggestion plays a major role in our lives. If you remain unaware of it, it will work against you more often than not. But if you decide to use it, all its tremendous power will be at your disposal."

"Well, I think you've convinced me to try," said the young man, "although, to tell you the truth, I'm still a little skeptical."

"That's all right. Just remember to base your judgment on the results, rather than on intellectual criteria. Now, come with me and I'll show you what to do."

# CHAPTER ELEVEN

*In which the young man
and his mentor discuss
figures and formulas*

THE MILLIONAIRE SAT DOWN AT THE DESK and invited the young man to join him. He took out some paper and a pen and wrote some figures.

"Your formula could look like this," he said. What he had written was, *By the end of this year I will possess assets worth $31,250. I will double those assets every year for five years, so that by* (and here he left a space) *I will be a millionaire.*

"You mustn't confuse assets and income," he told

the young man. "Your assets are whatever you have left over after your current bills and taxes are paid. Assets can comprise real estate investments, stocks or bonds, savings in banks or mutual funds, gold, art, jewelry, valuable collectibles, and so on. Now if you want to be a millionaire in six years — which is the realistic objective I'm proposing — your formula will have to be set up on this model. If you have assets worth $31,250 by the end of the first year, you will have to double them each year. And in six years you will be a millionaire!

"Why double your assets each year? *Because it's a simple operation that your subconscious can easily handle.* And it's easy for you to remember. It also guarantees you constant growth.

"If this starting point seems too ambitious for you, then give yourself another year. Becoming a millionaire in seven years is still pretty good! Your goal for the first year will then be to have assets of $15,625. Believe me when I tell you it's far from being beyond reach. If you're convinced that you can have a cozy nest egg worth $15,625 by the end of the first year, you *will* have it.

"Now if that still seems over-ambitious, give yourself yet another year, making a total of eight. Then the goal for your first year will be $7,812.50.

"Along with your formula and the affirmation *I will be a millionaire on* (put the month and year, in six, seven, or eight years' time), you will also have to set yourself short-term objectives, landmarks to help motivate you during your journey on the road to riches. And an annual goal is essential.

"The most important thing, however," he told his pupil, "is to write your goals down on paper. Take a pencil and fool around with figures and years. Don't be afraid; it can't do you any harm. The amounts will become more and more familiar to you as you play around with them. Millions of people want to get rich, and yet not one out of a hundred takes the initiative to outline the route he intends to take to reach his goal. Be different! Set up your plans and charts. Work out projections until you've found the plan that suits you. It'll be *your* plan.

"Use the examples I've provided for inspiration, but then let your imagination run wild. You have to start by dreaming to get rich. Then you have to know how to quantify your dream and translate it into specific sums of money and dates. This, in fact, should be the first exercise you do. Juggle numbers. You will soon see that this little game will reveal who you really are.

"The simple act of putting your goals, deadlines,

and sums on paper is the first step toward transforming your ideal into its material equivalent.

"Anyone who wants to stick to an ambition of becoming a millionaire in five or ten years must take note of this fact: If he is currently earning $35,000 a year and can expect nothing more than, say, an annual five or ten percent raise, and if he can save and invest only a small percentage of that, then he'll never become a millionaire if he remains in his job without sideline activities.

"There's nothing reprehensible in this; it's purely an objective observation. The formula of doubling your fortune each year or increasing your assets with respect to the previous years' is clearly not the only way to become a millionaire. However, the secret it contains, that is, a quantified goal (an amount and a deadline by which to reach it), is valid for anyone wishing to succeed in any way.

"For example, you might simply want to increase your income by $10,000 a year. If you now earn $35,000, you would probably like to earn $45,000 — a matter of affording a few more luxuries. Or perhaps you are earning $45,000 and would like $55,000 to enable you to trade up from your present house without worrying about the extra mortgage payments. Or you might want to be able to afford a new car, one that is a little more luxurious.

"To do this, simply repeat to yourself: *This year I will increase my income by $10,000 and I will earn $45,000.*

"You don't need to know how you'll manage it. You simply have to realize that if all you can hope for is a ten percent annual pay raise in your present job, and you don't want to moonlight, you will have to land a promotion or switch jobs to reach your goal. This may appear self-evident, but thousands of people hope to improve their material situation and do absolutely nothing about it. Is this ignorance? Is it because they are basically satisfied with their situations even though they complain day in and day out?

"Once you've discovered that you need some kind of change in your life to reach your goals, you might find yourself thinking that you have no other possibilities in sight. And you might wonder how the devil you're going to earn that extra $10,000 that you need. Don't worry; this isn't a serious dilemma. Just fully permeate your unconscious with your goal, duly written down stating such and such an amount and deadline. Your unconscious will do the rest. Then just stay on your toes. Since you've become aware that things won't get better on their own, when an opportunity arises, seize it without the slightest hesitation. Don't let yourself be paralyzed by fear, which prevents so many people from living out their dreams. You know that by doing nothing you won't get your raise. So you mustn't hesitate to take the steps necessary to achieve your goal.

"Correctly programmed, your unconscious will work wonders for you. If you've issued it the order to increase your income by $10,000, it will definitely execute it. Remind it daily, so your mission becomes its magnificent obsession. Like a remote-control missile, it will overcome all the obstacles in its way to hit its target.

"What is the target?" he continued. "When must the explosion take place? The target is $10,000 and the explosion date is a year from now. Such are the magical powers of the unconscious and a quantified objective.

"When creating your objectives, keep in mind that most people are much too cautious. They don't believe they're worth anything.

"A few years ago," he whispered confidentially to the young man, "I was thinking of hiring a managing director for one of my companies. I worked out that I'd be ready to offer him a salary of $100,000. When the time came to discuss his salary, he told me in a rather nervous, almost imperious voice: 'I won't accept anything below $70,000.'

"After a lengthy pause I said, as if I was making a

major concession: 'Given your background, $70,000 is fine by me.'

"If he had asked for $80,000 or $90,000, I'd have given it to him. In fact, the way the interview had gone pleased me so much I might even have bumped that amount up to $120,000.

"So the person I took on lost himself at least $30,000 in a matter of minutes. That's a lot of money. And he lost it simply because he didn't believe he was worth $100,000 a year. I must admit, after hearing him state his salary expectations, I hesitated for a second and considered not hiring him after all. He was in the best position to assess his own worth, and he was telling me that his managerial skills were worth only $70,000 while I was looking for someone worth $100,000. Was I making the wrong choice? The future proved I'd made the right choice by hiring him, and I saved a lot of money. His problem was that he lacked self-confidence and underestimated his worth. He gradually dealt with this problem over the years, and it cost me a bundle in salary increases. But they were worth it.

"What you should remember from this simple example is that I dealt with this manager just as life deals with each of us. Life gives us exactly what we expect from it. No more, no less. We tend to forget, however, that it is generally ready to give us much more than we realize.

"I've talked a lot," said the millionaire. "What do you make of all this, young man?"

"It seems too good to be true," he said.

"Yet this simple little method, and no other," the millionaire responded, "is exactly what helped turn me into a millionaire and has done the same for all those I've shared it with.

"As I've said, words are extremely powerful agents. The stronger your character becomes, the more the words you utter will become genuine decrees. Everything you affirm, fueled by deep inner conviction and strengthened by the fires of repetition, will take shape more and more quickly.

"You have to do the exercise. Nobody can do it for you. You must repeat your formula aloud day and night at least fifty times. And more if you can. Even a hundred times a day. This is an exercise in itself. The first few times I laid down and counted by tapping my fingers on the floor, five times with both hands. It takes practice.

"At first you'll find it won't be easy. The mind is prone to wander. After repeating it ten times, you'll start thinking of something else. Bring your mind back to business and start at zero again until you manage to reach fifty, because if you can't stick to such an elementary form of discipline, you'd better give up your dream of becoming rich.

"That's the challenge I'm offering you, my young friend. And I know you can do it. All you need to do is persist."

"Why repeat the formula aloud?"

"It affects your mind even more strongly. The order you are issuing to your unconscious seems as though it is coming from the outside, and thus sounds more commanding. Say it in a monotone, like an incantation or a mantra, as the Buddhists call it. In time the formula will acquire its own life.

"At first, you might feel a little embarrassed by the sound of your voice and by the formula you're repeating. But gradually you'll get used to it. The goal you laid out for yourself, which seemed audacious at first, will soon appear attainable, even easy to achieve."

"I'm afraid I might feel absolutely ridiculous."

"It's during those moments especially that you must persist. You must conquer your doubt. Think of me, living proof. Even if I'm in a garden far from here, my forces will be with you. In your moments of doubt, remember that I've given you my word. You *will* succeed."

"You're sure about that?" asked the young man, still not totally convinced.

"Why would I have any doubts about it? You'll become an instant millionaire like I did. It's only a matter of time before you become a millionaire in reality. You will soon be one in your mind, and that's what is most important."

"Even without a penny to my name...."

"Keep repeating the formula. Little by little you will see a change occurring within you. Your goal will seem more and more natural. It'll become part of your life in just the same way that the narrow image you have had of yourself until now — a well-worn figment of your imagination — has been an integral part of your being. What your mind conjured up in the past can be reformulated, so you will be able to mold your future the way you want it. You will at last become master of your own destiny. Isn't that our secret dream, even before we admit it's possible?"

The young man agreed, and was overwhelmed with emotion at the prospect of mastering his destiny. The old man's words had much greater significance than he had at first believed. Of course his methods were a bit strange. But perhaps they worked.

# CHAPTER TWELVE

*In which the young man learns about happiness and life*

T O HELP AND SUPPORT YOU," the Instant Millionaire told his young student, "I'll give you another more general formula. You'll derive enormous benefits from it throughout your life. It will transform you inside and out. In fact, it will enable you to acquire *true* wealth — which isn't only the acquisition of material possessions. True wealth is much broader than that.

"Your money formula will allow you to achieve

and probably even surpass your financial objectives. But during your search for wealth, never lose sight of the fact that if you lose happiness, you lose everything. The pursuit of money can easily turn into an obsession preventing you from enjoying life. And as the saying goes: 'What shall it profit a man, if he shall gain the whole world, and lose his soul?' Money is an excellent servant but a tyrannical master."

"Do you mean that happiness and money can't coexist?"

"Far from it, but you must stay very alert not to lose your perspective. One of the richest men in the world, John D. Rockefeller, was so preoccupied, so crushed by the weight of his worries, that by the age of fifty he was a little old man. His stomach was so out of order that all it could stand was bread and milk. He lived in constant fear of losing his money and being betrayed by his associates. Money had become his master. He couldn't enjoy it anymore. In a way he was poorer than a simple office clerk who could enjoy a good meal."

"At the same time that you're dangling wealth in front of my eyes," said the young man, "you manage to frighten me as well."

"That's not my intention, though," replied the millionaire, "and the formula I'm about to give you will help you avoid the trap many fortune-seekers have fallen into. People who are still basically poor work relentlessly to achieve their ends. The first money they earn triggers their deep-seated ambition, and causes them to crave more and more. And when they start earning big money they become afraid of losing it.

"It is a formula devised by the famous physician Emile Coué for patients in his clinic: *Every day, in every way, I'm getting better and better*. Repeat this formula aloud fifty times, morning and evening, and as many times as you can during the day. The more often you repeat it, the greater the impact it will have on you."

The young man found himself thinking that the man sitting next to him was the first truly happy man he had ever met in his life.

"Most people want to be happy," said the millionaire, "but they don't know what they're looking for. So inevitably they die without ever having found it. Even if they did find it, how would they recognize it? They're exactly like the people searching for wealth. They truly want to be rich. But when you ask them abruptly how much they'd like to earn in a year, most of them are incapable of answering. When you don't know where you're going, you generally get nowhere."

This made perfect sense to the young man. It was so disarmingly simple, he wondered why he'd never thought of it before. He'd never taken the time to clearly describe what he wanted, to really think things through. He vowed then and there that in the future he would do a lot more thinking, and reflect upon the things that mattered in his life. That would probably prevent a lot of mistakes.

"Happiness, of course, has been defined in countless different ways," the millionaire said. "For each of us, even for those of us who have given it much thought, it translates into a wide variety of things. But I'll give you the key to happiness. With this key you will be able to know beyond a shadow of a doubt at any time of your life if you are happy, if you are doing what it takes to make you happy. Ask yourself this: If I were to die tonight, could I tell myself at the instant of my death that I had accomplished everything I had set out to do that day?

"When you have done exactly what your inner self feels you should do each day, you will feel free to leave the world each day. To be perfectly sure that you are doing what you should be doing, you will have to do what you love doing. People who don't do what they enjoy are not happy. They spend their time day-dreaming about what they would like to be doing.

And when people aren't happy, they aren't ready to die at a moment's notice."

"I've barely started living, and here you go talking to me about death as if it were just around the corner," the young man said.

"I admit this philosophy may seem morbid at first. And yet it's a philosophy of *life*, one hundred percent. Those who never do what they really enjoy doing, who have given up their dreams, so to speak, belong to the living dead. To really understand what I mean, ask yourself that question and answer it with total sincerity. If you lie, you'll only be lying to yourself, and you become the loser in this game. If you knew you were going to die tomorrow, wouldn't you change your plans for today? Wouldn't you do something else with your life rather than what you've been doing up to now?"

"I'm sure I would."

"You'd probably start by making the necessary arrangements: you'd make a will, if you hadn't already, and say good-bye to your family and friends. But let's suppose that all of these tasks took only one hour. What would you do with the remaining twenty-three? Ask that question of everybody you know. Their responses will invariably fall into two categories. Unhappy people who don't enjoy their lives will tell you that they'd do something totally different. Why on earth would they continue doing something they hated if they had only twenty-four hours left to live?

"Those in the second category," he continued, "and unfortunately they're the minority, would do exactly what they normally do every day of their lives. Why would they change anything? Their work is their passion. Isn't it quite understandable they would do it until their time was up? Bach belonged to this category. One his deathbed he was correcting his last piece of music. But you don't have to be a genius to want to work until the end. Each of us in our own way and in our own occupation can become a genius, even if unrecognized as such by society. *To be a genius simply means to do what you enjoy doing. That is the true genius of life.* Mediocrity is never daring to do what you love, for fear of what others will say or for fear of losing your security."

"A security that is an illusion more often than not, isn't it?" asked the young man.

"That's right. So ask yourself the question: If I were to die tomorrow, what would I do with the last hours of my life? Would I agree to go on being a shadow of my true self, lacking in self-respect, forcing myself to do something I hate? Imagine you invite a friend over to your house to help you do some chores. Would you give the dirtiest ones to your friend? Of course not. So why force on yourself tasks that you find so degrading? Why be your own worst enemy? Why not become your own best friend?"

There was a moment of silence, and then the old millionaire asked the young man directly. "And what would you do if you were to die tomorrow? Would you do exactly what you've been doing?"

"No, I wouldn't."

"Now, consider the following observation. Don't you find it highly presumptuous to believe that you won't die tomorrow?"

The young man felt troubled. The old man had often displayed an uncanny ability to see into the future — was he now announcing his imminent death? The millionaire seemed to read his thoughts.

"Don't worry," he said, obviously amused, "you're not going to die tomorrow. You'll live to a ripe old age. But allow me to pursue my line of reasoning. Don't you find it presumptuous of people to believe that they always have their entire lives ahead of them? In many cases, death strikes out of the blue. But people create the illusion that they have lots of time ahead of them, and they constantly put off the decisions they should make. They tell themselves: 'I've got time. I'll get down to business later.' Then old age arrives and they find they haven't done anything yet."

"It reminds me of a saying I heard: 'If youth only knew, if old age only could,'" said the young man.

"Exactly! The secret of happiness, therefore, is to live as if each day was your last. And to live each day to the fullest by doing what you want to do. What you would do if your hours were numbered. Because, realistically, they are. We always seem to realize this when there's very little time left. Then it's too late. So *you must be courageous enough to act immediately*. Live with this thought in mind: I refuse to die without having had the courage to do what I wanted to do. I don't want to die with the appalling thought that society tricked me, that it got the better of me and annihilated my dreams. You must not die with the dreadful feeling that your fears were greater than your dreams and that you never discovered what you really enjoy. *You must know how to dare*."

"I totally agree," said the young man, "but what happens if I'm not absolutely sure that I don't really like what I'm doing? I don't know of any occupation that's completely free of hassles."

"You're absolutely right. Even a profession that fires us up has its negative aspects. But to find out whether your job *really* pleases you, ask yourself this question: If I had a million dollars in the bank, right at this moment, would I continue doing the same job? Obviously, if your answer is no, you don't like it enough. Tell me, how many people would continue in the same occupation if they suddenly became millionaires? They are few and far between. And those who would answer yes to this question are generally already millionaires. Most of the millionaires I know refuse to retire. They go on working very late in life. I'd even go so far as to say that all millionaires, at least all self-made millionaires, made their fortunes precisely because they loved their work.

"My reasoning has just come full circle," the millionaire said. "To become a millionaire, you must enjoy your occupation. Those who stay in a job they hate are doubly penalized. Not only do they despise their work, but, worse yet, it doesn't even make them wealthy. In fact, most people spend their lives in this strange paradox. Why? Because they are unaware of the genuine laws of success, and because of fear. They waste their lives and their chances of becoming truly rich by clinging to a type of security that is mediocre at best. They believe wealth is reserved for others, or that they don't have the necessary talent. And why do they let themselves be tricked into believing these illusions? Because their minds are not conditioned to see reality, to see that their beliefs are an illusion. Remember the saying: 'Character equals destiny.' Strengthen your mind, and circumstances will yield to your desires. You will gain control over your own life."

"Have you always been happy?" asked the young man.

"No, not at all. There were times when I was absolutely miserable. The thought of committing suicide even crossed my mind. But then I, too, met an eccentric old millionaire who taught me almost everything I'm telling you today. At first I was pretty skeptical. I couldn't believe this theory could apply in my case, even though he was living proof that it worked. But since I had tried all sorts of things and was still unsuccessful, and since I had nothing to lose, I was willing to give it a try. I was thirty and I felt I was wasting my life. It seemed as if things were slipping through my fingers."

"I'm sure that today you don't regret having taken the advice."

"He often said I could become the master of my life and control all the events taking place in it. But I never believed him; it seemed like science fiction. Then, one day, after hearing him repeat the same song over and over again, I told myself that maybe he was right. Maybe life was not what I'd always thought it was: a series of more or less unpredictable and un-controllable events in which luck or fate ruled. Maybe it was possible that we could control our destinies if we mastered our minds. Soon I was beginning to think like that; in other words, a revolution was taking place in my mind. It happened only after I'd spent quite some time repeating to myself: *Every day, in every way, I'm getting better and better.*

"My mentor also taught me another formula, which in my opinion is even more powerful — at least as far as my own experience goes — and I highly rec-ommend it to you. It's slightly religious in nature, which puts some people off. But that's a pity, since it has an invaluable effect on the mind. Repeating this formula has calmed me down when I felt anxious or nervous and has brought me answers when I seriously needed them. Tranquility is the greatest manifesta-tion of power.

"*Be still, and know that I am God.* Repeat it every day as often as you can. It will bring you that feeling of serenity so necessary for getting through life's up-heavals. When my mentor decided to reveal it to me, he said that of all the secrets in the world, this one was the most precious. It was his spiritual legacy to me, as it is mine to you.

"By repeating this formula, which seemed strange to me at first, I developed a new inner power. This power, which never ceased growing over the years, kept reminding me of something the old millionaire had repeated to me over and over again: *I could do anything*; nothing would be impossible for me as soon as I became the master of my destiny. So, little by little, I convinced myself that I could steer my life exactly where I wanted it to go. I've continued applying the formula and I want you to do the same thing."

# CHAPTER THIRTEEN

*In which the young man learns*
*to express his desires in life*

"Y OU HAVE ALREADY TAKEN THE FIRST STEP," explained the millionaire, "writing the formula and the quantified objective: an amount and a deadline. Now for the second step: take a sheet of paper and write down everything you want out of life. Your dream must be precise if you want it to take shape. I'll show you what I asked for in the beginning. It was many years ago, so I'll translate the amounts roughly into today's dollars:

"The following financial goals within five years:

- A house worth $750,000.
- A second home in the country worth $500,000.
- A new BMW worth $80,000.
- An old, rebuilt Mercedes worth $50,000.
- No more personal debts.
- $500,000 in cash and other liquid assets.
- $500,000 invested in the stock market and other investments.
- $500,000 invested in property, which grows to $3,000,000 in equity within five years from the time of purchase.

"My non-financial objectives were:

- Two-week vacations at least three times a year, whenever I felt like taking them.
- To be my own boss and not work more than thirty hours a week.
- Intelligent friends involved in business and art.
- A loving and charming wife and beautiful children; a fulfilling family life.
- A maid and cook to free us of everyday tasks."

The young man was overwhelmed by the picture the Instant Millionaire had just drawn.

"It looks too good to be true, doesn't it?" said the millionaire. "I too thought that I'd gone a bit overboard by the time I'd finished outlining what I wanted.

But my hesitation and fears were due to a negative mental attitude and my ingrained habit of thinking small. I was doing this without even realizing it.

"Making out a list like this is exactly the way to discover your narrow vision of things. Those who consider this kind of life plan unachievable simply think small. Everything being relative under the sun, this ambition is hardly exorbitant. Most wealthy people would be exceedingly unhappy if they had to make do with the paltry conditions I have just sketched out. Many of them live in houses worth millions, employ dozens of servants, and own ranches, private planes, tropical islands, racehorses, and so on. Many of them don't even think they're rich! In any case not *that* rich, since they always have friends or business associates with more money than they have.

"Why do they find this kind of lifestyle natural? Well, either they were born rich, or they thought big and managed to achieve their dreams. They never believed that they couldn't do it. If you start out with the idea that you can't, you immediately block yourself.

"So, do this exercise. Write down what you want out of life in minute detail, without holding anything back. It will show you the limits of your ambitions and your mentality. What are you really dreaming of? What would you be satisfied with? It's important to fill in as many details as possible. The only thing to avoid is choosing your dream home at a specific address, because that particular house may never be available and you'd be running the risk of never seeing your dream come true despite the power of your desire and will. But other than that, be as specific as possible.

"There's one other important thing to consider, and that is the possibility that your dream is harmful to others. Always keep in mind that if your goals are harmful to anyone, they must be avoided for your own good as well as for the good of others.

"This portrait will show you who you really are. It will become the concrete shape of your desires. Your thoughts are alive. The more specific your portrait, the better the chances are for it to materialize. Details are very important. In mysterious and unexpected ways your thoughts, nourished regularly, bring about the circumstances that allow them to become reality."

The young man looked a bit skeptical.

"I know all this seems Utopian," the millionaire said. "But as I told you, the stronger your mind becomes, the more you realize there's nothing it can't accomplish. Miracles happen. Don't you find that, comparatively speaking, realizing a dream as ordinary as having a $750,000 house is a rather banal achievement? Don't you believe that the mind is much more powerful than many people think and above all believe it to be? Remember what Christ said: 'Faith moves mountains.'

"To use your mind effectively, you've got to start believing in its power, or at least be open to the possibility that it might be as powerful as I'm telling you it is. So draw up your list."

"I need time to think," said the young man.

"That's good. Think about what I've just told you. Part of you believes what I'm saying. A highly creative part of you has been blinded by years of faulty education and unfortunate experiences, but it's still alive. It's only waiting for a sign from you, and it will show you how to become the lord and master of your existence instead of a tormented slave helplessly buffeted by events. To do that you must learn to listen to that tiny inner voice sleeping in the depths of your mind and give it more freedom to express itself. This is your intuition, the voice of your soul. It's the way to your secret power. The more often you repeat the formula *Be still, and know that I am God*, the more powerful your inner voice will become and the more surely it will guide you."

The young man felt a bit overloaded; he was ready to take a break.

"Come," said the millionaire, "let's relax and take a walk in the garden. I'd love to take my last walk here with a friend."

These somber words saddened the young man. It wasn't the first time he had made such an allusion. . . .

## CHAPTER FOURTEEN

## *In which the young man discovers the secrets of the rose garden*

THE TWO MEN WALKED THROUGH THE GARDEN in silence until the millionaire stopped in front of a rose bush laden with magnificent flowers.

"I must have smelled these roses thousands of times, and yet each time it's a different experience. Do you know why? Because I've learned to live in the here and now, and not dwell on the past or the future. It's a matter of mental concentration — focusing, contemplation, meditation — a great many words have been used to describe it. The more you concentrate on what you are doing, absorbed in the task or object or person in front of you, the more you live in the present. This focus, this concentration, is a key to success in all facets of life. The better your concentration, the more quickly and efficiently you're able to work. You'll spot details that others overlook."

"Have all rich and successful people learned to pay attention to details?"

"They have indeed. By increasing your own powers of concentration, you will be able to make wise observations. You will learn to judge accurately the people you meet. Your powers of concentration will enable you to discover at a glance who they really are. And you will become realistic in the truest sense of the word: You will see things as they are.

"Most people go through life constantly distracted, like sleepwalkers. They don't really *see* things or *see* the people they meet. They live as if in a dream. They are never in the present. Their mistakes and failures haunt them. Their minds are filled with fears of the future."

"I have a feeling that concentration, as you're describing it, is quite a difficult thing to achieve."

"It takes practice, and not everyone who tries it succeeds. But when your mind reaches a proper level of concentration, your ability to solve problems becomes formidable. You can leap over problems most people dwell on. Instead of wasting your nervous energy biting your nails over your worries, you apply yourself to resolving them. Being overanxious never solved anything — it simply provoked many a stomach ulcer and heart attack.

"As you develop your forces of concentration, the image you have of yourself will change. Each human being is an enigma; unfortunately, many of us are enigmas not only to others, but to ourselves as well. This comes from a lack of concentration."

The young man was listening intently.

"Given concentration, you will understand why you've been placed where you are in the world, in this exact spot. This will appear clearer and clearer to you, more and more obvious. Your mind will be penetrated by very calming, reassuring thoughts, and you'll find yourself realizing, as if waking up after a long, deep sleep, 'Ah! That's who I am. That's why I'm here at this moment. That's why I'm with this person. That's why I'm doing what I'm doing.' You'll experience what could be called a feeling of destiny. You'll understand your destiny. And a feeling of acceptance will come into play. That doesn't mean you resign yourself to fate; it means you will see with clear-sighted vision the position you're in right now, you'll accept it, and you'll recognize it as your personal starting point. This will guide your career and allow you to take the reins of your destiny firmly in your hands."

The millionaire took a moment to bend down and inhale the perfume of the rose.

"The rose is a symbol of life. The thorns represent the road of experience: the trials and tribulations each one of us must undergo to understand the true beauty of existence."

He pulled a pair of pruning shears out of his pocket, snipped a rose, and offered it to his young companion.

"Keep this rose with you," he said. "It will act as a talisman and bring you good luck. Lady Luck exists. Trust in her. Caress her with your thoughts. Ask her for what you want and she will respond. All successful people believe in luck, in one form or another.

"With this simple rose, you are an initiate. You belong to the Order of the Rose. Each time you feel the need, find this rose. It will give you strength. And each time you have doubts about yourself, each time life seems too difficult to bear, come back to this symbolic rose and remember what it represents. Each ordeal, each problem, each mistake will one day be transformed into a magnificent petal.

"Each day, set aside some time to concentrate on the heart of the rose. Repeat calmly to yourself: *Be still, and know that I am God*. Contemplate the rose for longer and longer periods of time while repeating this. When you are able to do it for twenty minutes, your concentration will be much improved.

"When your heart becomes like the rose, your life will be transformed."

The young man breathed in the delicate scent of the rose.

"Let me repeat what I have said, so you are sure to remember. When your mind has become strong and self-assured through concentration exercises, you will come to realize that life's problems no longer have any hold over you. You will understand that things are only as important as the mind believes them to be. A problem is a problem only if you make it a problem.

"The stronger your mind is, the more insignificant your problems appear. This is the source of inner peace, so *concentrate*. This is one of the greatest keys to success.

"All of life is an exercise in strengthening the mind. The soul is immortal. We pass from life to life, and the mind slowly discovers itself and develops. This apprenticeship is generally a long one. And people who have no more than modest success in reaching their goals have yet to achieve high levels of concentration. Perhaps not all successful people have made it a point to practice specific concentration exercises. But over the course of many lives on earth they have achieved a level of concentration that allowed them to succeed more easily than others. When your mind reaches its highest level of concentration, you will enter that extraordinary state where dreams and reality coincide."

The millionaire and the young man began walking back to the house. The sky became dark and cloudy, casting shadows over the mansion. When they entered the dining room, the old man lit a candelabra. Then he went to the window, pulled the curtain back, and glanced up toward the sky.

"Always remember that at a certain height there are no clouds. If there are clouds in your life, it's because your soul hasn't soared high enough.

"Many people make the mistake of fighting against their problems. What you must do is raise yourself above those problems once and for all. The heart of the rose will lead you above the clouds, where the sky is forever clear. Don't waste your time chasing the clouds; they will unceasingly reappear...."

The millionaire and the young man sat down at the dinner table. The butler arrived, bringing bread and wine.

"I've been wondering about something for quite a while," said the young man. "I do think everything you've been saying is true. And I now believe that if I apply the formulas you've given me, I can become a millionaire quickly and even attain peace of mind. But I still wonder about the *field* in which I'll be able to make a fortune."

His concern apparently amused the millionaire.

"You must put your trust in life and in the power of your mind," he said. "Don't worry. First set your goal, then ask your deep unconscious to steer you toward the path that will lead to riches. Start by asking; then wait. The answer won't be long in coming."

The young man was disappointed. He wanted something a little more specific.

The millionaire winced in sympathy and quickly added: "You must find work that is satisfying to your heart. Think about it. All the elements of the occupation that will please you are already within you. You simply don't recognize them because you aren't yet in tune with your true nature. As you continue to concentrate, to meditate more and more, you will connect with your true essence, and every answer you need will be revealed to you. And best of all, you will discover what most people desperately seek all their lives and never find: the mysterious purpose of your existence on earth. And you will understand it not only with your head but with your heart as well.

"You have everything to gain from concentrating on the heart of the rose. There you will find the be-all and end-all of your existence. In time, you will realize this."

He stopped for a moment and took a tiny sip of wine, delicately savoring it. His eyes were closed in a kind of religious reverence.

"I know I would like to start a business of some kind," said the young man, "but where would I get the money to start? I haven't got a dime."

"How much would you need?"

"I don't know — at least $25,000. That's how much you needed to start."

"You should be able to find it. Look around a little. What possibilities can you think of?"

"I can't think of any. I don't know of any bank that would give me a loan. I have no collateral. I have very little left over from my salary at the end of the month, and I don't own anything except my car, which isn't worth anything...."

"Can't you at least think of something to try? Somewhere to begin?"

"Not really...."

"That's a mistake you should never repeat. Don't be like so many people, who give up before they even try. That's the best way of never doing anything and never succeeding at anything. And don't fall into the same trap as those who take action but are inwardly convinced that they won't succeed. Bring your thoughts and actions into harmony. Be in harmony with yourself."

"I'm willing all right, but I just don't see any possibilities."

"You must start out firmly convinced that the solution exists — the ideal solution to your problem. The power of your mind and the magic of your objective will invariably attract the solution to you in ways you don't even suspect exist. Be inwardly convinced that you will succeed, and you will. Don't leave room for doubt. Banish it with all the strength your mind can muster. Doubt and optimism are in constant conflict. Struggle staunchly against doubt, for doubt, like all thoughts, tends to materialize in your life. If you are firmly convinced that you will get your loan, you will.

"In your present circumstances, what would you do to reach your goal — that is, to get a loan?"

"I don't really know."

"If you only had a short time — let's say an hour — to get $25,000 to set up your own business, what would you do?"

"I . . . I have no idea. . . ."

"Standing before you is a millionaire who has just encouraged you, given you the secrets of his success, and you don't know what to do? Not one thing comes to mind to get this money?"

It suddenly dawned on the young man. Perhaps all he needed to do was ask the millionaire for the money. He hesitated a moment, then took a deep breath.

"Would you lend me the $25,000 I need?"

"There you go. Now, wasn't that easy? All you had to do was ask. People seldom dare to ask. *You must dare to make a request.*"

The millionaire pulled out the $25,000 he kept as pocket money. He cast a nostalgic glance at the thick pile of cash and then handed it over to the young man, who accepted it, tremulous with emotion. He had never held such a vast sum of money in his life.

"There's absolutely no reason why acquiring money in the future should be any more difficult for you than it has been for me," said the old man. "It's unfortunate that it's so commonly believed that money is hard to come by and that you have to work hard to get it. In fact, the value of work is to strengthen the fiber of your mind. When you have earned a lot of money — and I assure you it won't be long in coming if you apply the secrets I've taught you — you will realize that what counts is your mental attitude, the power of your desire, and being able to channel that power by means of a specific monetary objective. Don't forget that outside circumstances always end up reflecting the state of your mind and the nature of your innermost convictions."

The young man was so overcome with joy at having $25,000 in his hands that he wasn't fully listening to the millionaire's words of advice.

"Remember, young man, when you need money, if you are positive you can get it easily and quickly, you will. And as soon as doubt begins to invade your mind, think back to the $25,000 you've just obtained. All you need to do is ask. If you are convinced that you will get what you ask for at the very moment you ask, if you act as if it is already yours, you will get it.

"When you do have doubts, apply some self-suggestion. Turn your words into commands. When your mind has become powerful enough, each suggestion will become a royal decree. Your words and reality will become one. And the time it takes for your commands to materialize will become briefer and briefer, and finally instantaneous.

"And you must never forget to consider the good of others at all times, so that the power of your words doesn't turn against you."

He paused again.

"This money," he went on, pointing to the thick wad of bills, "well, I'm not lending it to you. . . ."

He hesitated a second, and seemed amused by the young man's startled reaction.

"I'm not lending it to you. I'm giving it to you. By my doing so, everything will have come full circle. It was given to me by my mentor to start me out in business. Don't use it for any other reason. And don't imitate the man in the Bible who buried his coins instead of letting them work for him. Don't let fear be your guide. Fear is your worst enemy, the brother of doubt, and you must conquer it. Be fearless and bold. Anyone who, under the pretext of caution or rationality, buries the money he has received is not worthy of it, and it's highly unlikely that he will get more. Money must flow freely to be able to multiply.

"The money I'm giving you is, however, at heart a loan," the millionaire continued. "One day you, in turn, must give it to someone else. Many years from now you will meet someone in the same situation you are in now. You'll recognize him intuitively. You must give him the equivalent of what this amount represents today. Then he, too, may start out with a substantial amount. Make sure that by then it represents an insignificant amount to you: pocket money and no more."

The young man was filled with gratitude. He agreed to the terms, and thanked the old man warmly.

"There's one more thing you must know. . . ."

As he said this, it began to pour. The millionaire watched the rain with a somber expression. "All the signs are coming to pass," he muttered to himself. Then he addressed the young man again.

"As I said, there's one more thing you need to know: The secrets I have passed on to you are effective for reaching *all* of the goals you will set for yourself. The reason I amassed such a colossal fortune is not that money interested me so much. It was a way to show men and women of little faith the power of the mind.

"Our greatest possession is freedom, and wealth can give you freedom. It'll be good for you to know this freedom. With it, you will see many an illusion vanish. You'll also understand that true freedom is found in detachment. Only he who leaves with empty hands will be able to tend the eternal roses. Achieving this freedom was the goal of my entire existence. Despite what others thought, I have never been anything other than a humble gardener."

"Why have you told *me* all these things?" the young man asked. "Why have you given *me* this money? You certainly didn't owe me anything. It could easily have been somebody else who came to see you...."

"But that's just it — no one else came. Your desire led you to me. This is what happens in life. Hasn't it been said that once the disciple is ready, the master appears?"

The millionaire smiled. His somber and distant expression disappeared; he looked at the young man affectionately.

"The soul is eternal. And each soul travels from one life to another surrounded by companions, each helping another to fulfill his destiny. The encounters we have during our lifetime are never the result of coincidence."

The millionaire approached him regally. His face almost seemed to glow with a light of its own. He lightly touched the young man on the forehead with his right index finger and said, "Discover who you really are. The truth will forever set you free."

Outside, the storm subsided as quickly as it had begun, and the sun burst forth brightly again. The old man picked up the candelabra and carried it away without saying another word.

The young man found himself alone, his head teeming with thoughts, holding the money the millionaire had given him.

## CHAPTER FIFTEEN

*In which the young man
and the old man embark
on different journeys*

T HE YOUNG MAN WAS NOT ALONE FOR LONG.
The butler appeared, holding an envelope. He
handed it to the young man and said, "My master en-
trusted me with the task of giving this to you. He said
you should read it in the privacy of your room. You
may spend another day here. Then you must go.
These are my master's wishes."

The young man thanked him and went immediately

to his room. This time, however, he took the precaution of leaving the door slightly open. . . .

The envelope was sealed with red wax in the shape of a rose. The young man sat on the edge of the bed and carefully broke the seal. A delicate scent of roses wafted from it. He pulled out the Instant Millionaire's will.

This extraordinary testament was handwritten in ample, majestic letters that seemed to breathe as if imbued with their own life. A beautifully handwritten letter accompanied it, written in black ink.

"These are my last requests," he read. "I am leaving you all the books in my library. Some people believe that books are utterly worthless. They believe that they themselves are reinventing the world. And since they have not benefited from the knowledge found in books, they unfortunately repeat the mistakes made by their forefathers. In this way, they waste a lot of time and a lot of money.

"On the other hand, don't fall into the trap of trusting implicitly in what books contain, letting those who came before you do your thinking for you. Retain only what outlasts the passage of time.

"Since our first encounter, I have tried to convey to you the pearls of wisdom I have been able to glean during my long life. In this document you will find a few thoughts that represent my spiritual legacy. I would like you to do your best to communicate them to as many people as you can. Tell people about our encounter and the secrets you have learned. Before doing so, however, you must try them out. A method that has not been tested and proven in your own experience is completely worthless.

"Within six years you will be a millionaire. At that time you will be free to undertake the steps necessary to share this legacy with people.

"Now I must leave you. My roses are waiting."

The young man was choked with emotion, and sat for a moment in silence.

He wanted to thank the millionaire for having given him such precious gifts. He went quickly back to the dining room, but found no one. He called out to the butler, but there was no answer.

He ran out to the garden and spotted the millionaire lying in the middle of a path at the foot of a rose bush.

"How eccentric," thought the young man, "sleeping in the middle of a garden." But the nearer he drew, the more troubled he became.

The old man's hands were folded upon his chest, and he held a single rose. His face was perfectly serene.

Had he known the exact moment he was going to die? Had he chosen the moment of his departure, and simply willed himself to die?

It was one secret the millionaire had taken with him.

The young man sensed it was time for him, too, to leave. He reached to take the rose, but then pulled his hand away. That rose belonged to the Instant Millionaire. It was his final companion.

He stood over the millionaire and vowed to convey his teachings as best he could, then started down the path to return home.

When the millionaire's library was delivered to his apartment, it was so immense it left little room for the rest of his things. He was confronted with a dilemma: either move elsewhere or get rid of some of the books. He chose to move. And he did it with a light heart.

# EPILOGUE

J UST AS THE MILLIONAIRE HAD PREDICTED, the young man made his first million before his six-year deadline was up. And he kept his promise: He took a month off and wrote about his encounter with the Instant Millionaire and the life-giving philosophy he had passed on to him.